THE NORTHUMBERLAND COAST

PHOTOGRAPHY
GRAEME PEACOCK

TEXT
PAUL FRODSHAM

NORTHERN
HERITAGE

Northern Heritage,
Units 7&8 New Kennels, Blagdon Estate, Seaton Burn,
Newcastle upon Tyne NE13 6DB
Telephone: 01670 789 940
www.northern-heritage.co.uk

ISBN No.978-0-9555406-0-8

Printed and bound in China by 1010 Printing International Limited.

British Library Cataloguing in Publishing Data
A catalogue record for this book is available from the British Library.

Also available in this series:

Places featured in this book are managed and interpreted for the public
by a combination of agencies including English Heritage, the National
Trust, local authorities, conservation charities and private landowners.
When visiting them, please treat them with respect and avoid damaging
ancient monuments (eg by climbing on walls) or disturbing natural
habitats. Details of opening times, admission charges etc are available from
tourist information centres.

GRAEME PEACOCK

Graeme Peacock is one of the best known and highly regarded photographers of landscapes and architecture in the North of England. A former Town Planner, born 'n bred on Tyneside, Graeme has for over 20 years built up a stock in excess of 49,000 stunning colour images of our region. Regular clients include The National Trust, English Heritage, Ordnance Survey and The Royal Mail. To see more Graeme Peacock images visit his website www.graeme-peacock.com

INTRODUCTION

Wild, lonely windswept beaches; dramatic cliffs; ancient castles and monasteries; attractive little harbours and seaside resorts; breeding sites for thousands of seabirds and seals: the Northumberland coast has an abundance of everything a coastline should have. From Berwick-upon-Tweed in the north to Tynemouth in the south, there is something very special about the entire length of this coast, resulting from unique combinations of landscape, nature and history. The landscape is essentially low-lying, but outcrops of hard volcanic rock, part of the great Whin Sill, provide rocky promontories and spectacular sea cliffs at Bamburgh, on the Farne Islands and elsewhere. Although the landscape has evolved over hundreds of millions of years, the present coastline is relatively recent, only forming from about 10,000 years ago as sea levels rose at the end of the last Ice Age: prior to this people could walk freely over much of what is now the North Sea. Archaeologists have recovered evidence of people who lived near the coast by hunting and fishing nearly 10,000 years ago, and fishing has been an important aspect of life here ever since.

Despite Northumberland's treacherous coastal waters, which have claimed countless lives over the centuries, the sea has always provided vital trading and communication links with other parts of Britain and with Europe. Indeed, the coast has played a key role in Northumbrian history. It was at Bamburgh that Ida landed in 547 to found the great Anglian dynasty that ruled the Kingdom of Northumbria, covering much of northern England and southern Scotland in the latter half of the first millennium. Within this kingdom, during its so-called 'Golden Age' of the 7th and 8th centuries, Christianity thrived, linked with figures such as Cuthbert, Aidan, Wilfred and Bede. Important monasteries were founded at Lindisfarne and Tynemouth, linked by sea to Rome and other key places in the early Christian world. This was a time of great cultural and artistic achievement, symbolised by the magnificent Lindisfarne Gospels, produced on Holy Island in about 700.

Lindisfarne was sacked by Vikings in 793, and, under constant threat of further

such attacks, Northumberland's early monasteries were abandoned during the 9th century. After the Norman Conquest of 1066, Lindisfarne and Tynemouth monasteries were refounded and survived through until the Dissolution in the 1530s. As well as their monasteries, the Normans were very fond of building great castles, such as Bamburgh, Berwick and Warkworth. These castles saw much active service during the Anglo-Scottish border wars of the 14th, 15th and 16th centuries, and Berwick's 16th century town defences are regarded as some of the finest in Europe. Although some later defensive structures were provided against sea-borne threats from France and Spain (and, more recently, Germany), the generally more peaceful conditions following the Union of the Crowns in 1603 enabled the development of many attractive coastal towns and villages, all of which contribute in their own way to our unique coastal heritage.

The northern half of the coast, from the Tweed to the Coquet, is designated as an Area of Outstanding Natural Beauty: it is thus officially recognised and protected as one of England's most treasured rural landscapes. In contrast, the land to the south of the Coquet has seen much industrial activity and, due in part to its proximity to Newcastle, has a much higher density of settlement. In the 19th century, Blyth was a major seaport and ship-building centre, engaged, like many of the smaller ports, in the export of coal from the vast Northumbrian coalfields. Following the decline in these traditional heavy industries, much has been done to improve the landscape. At Druridge Bay, following an ambitious programme of environmental work, old coal-workings have been landscaped to form important habitats for seabirds and other wildlife. The Northumbrian coast is famous for its seabirds which nest in vast numbers on the Farne Islands, Lindisfarne, Coquet Island and several mainland sites. The Farne Islands also provide an important breeding site for seals.

This collection of Graeme Peacock's beautiful photographs demonstrates why Northumbrians regard their coast with such affection. In the words of celebrated broadcaster Brian Redhead, *'New every morning is the love that people have for these shores, and Cuthbert would still recognize the place.'*

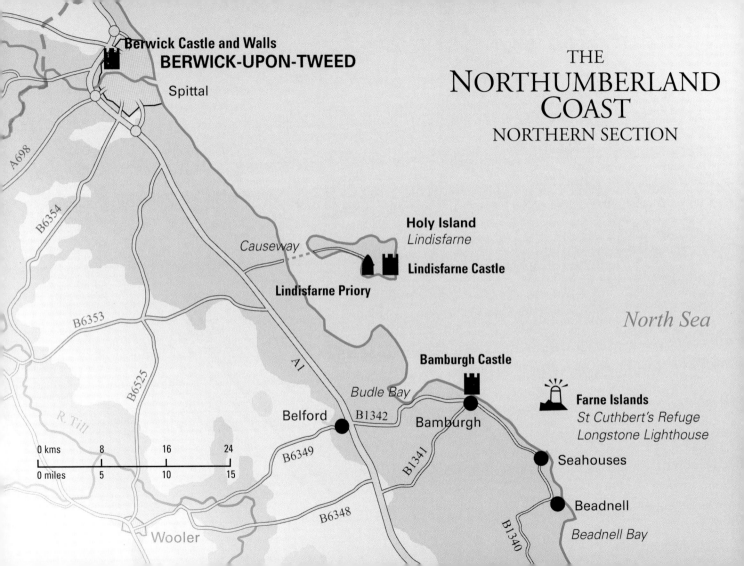

Berwick Castle and Walls
BERWICK-UPON-TWEED
Spittal

THE
NORTHUMBERLAND
COAST
NORTHERN SECTION

A698

B6354

Causeway

Holy Island
Lindisfarne

Lindisfarne Castle

Lindisfarne Priory

B6353

North Sea

B6525

A1

Bamburgh Castle

R. Till

Budle Bay

Farne Islands
St Cuthbert's Refuge
Longstone Lighthouse

Belford

B1342

Bamburgh

0 kms		8		16		24
0 miles		5		10		15

B6349

B1341

Seahouses

B1340

Beadnell

B6348

Wooler

Beadnell Bay

Berwick-upon-Tweed's unique heritage arises from its location on the much-disputed Anglo-Scottish border. During the 12th and 13th centuries the town, on the north bank of the Tweed, became prosperous as a Scottish port through which wool, hides and other goods were exported. Edward I captured it for England at the outset of the Border Wars in 1296, after which massive defences were constructed around the town. Despite these defences, Berwick was retaken for the Scots by Robert the Bruce in 1318, after which it changed hands a dozen times before becoming 'permanently' English in 1482. In the early 16th century, Berwick's old medieval defences were adapted to protect the town from Scottish artillery, and a little later, under Elizabeth I, they were completely redesigned. After the Union of the Crowns in 1603, Berwick's strategic importance dwindled and the defences became redundant: they survive largely intact as a unique legacy of the border's turbulent medieval history. By the 18th century Berwick was again a thriving port, and many fine 18th and 19th century buildings contribute to the unique character of what is regarded by many experts as one of Britain's most fascinating towns.

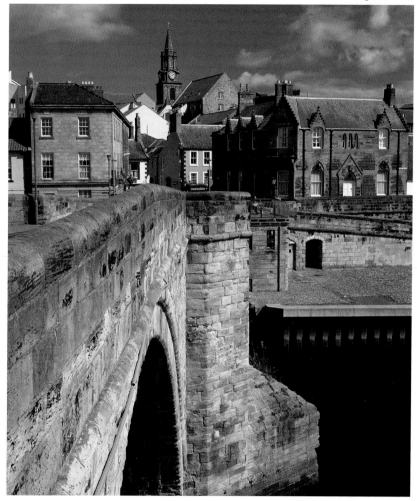

Berwick-upon-Tweed.

Christmas lights, Berwick-upon-Tweed.

Berwick Castle, dating originally from the 12th century, was left outside the town walls and was linked to the north bank of the Tweed by the still impressive White Wall, built in 1297-8. The castle was abandoned after the Union of the Crowns, but impressive ruins survived through until the mid 18th century, at which point they were largely blasted away in the name of progress, to make way for the railway station. Although sadly responsible for wrecking the castle, the railway did provide one magnificent addition to the town's architecture: the stunning Royal Border Bridge, designed by Robert Stephenson and completed in 1850.

The White Wall, Berwick-upon-Tweed.

Lindisfarne (Holy Island) is the best known of Northumberland's early Christian sites. A monastery was established here by King Oswald and St Aidan in 635. This was sacked by Vikings in 793, and, under constant threat of further attack, was eventually abandonded in 875. Today's spectacular ruins belong to the late 11th century Priory, founded on the same site by the Bishop of Durham, which remained in use through until the Dissolution when much of its stonework was pillaged by the builders of Lindisfarne Castle. The castle dates originally from 1550, but owes much of its present day appearance to the architect Sir Edwin Lutyens, who transformed it from a ruined shell into a splendid house in the early 20th century.

Lindisfarne (Holy Island) from the mainland.

Lindisfarne Priory and Castle.

Above: **St Aidan's statue, Lindisfarne.**

Left: **St Aidan's statue and Lindisfarne Castle.**

In addition to its cultural heritage, Lindisfarne is a nature reserve with important plants, birds and sealife. There are many fascinating places to explore here, information about which is available at the excellent Lindisfarne Heritage Centre. But be warned! Always check the tide tables when planning a visit as the causeway to the island is submerged at high tide and closed for several hours each day.

*Above: **Pilgrims crossing the causeway, Lindisfarne.***
*Right: **Causeway refuge hut, Lindisfarne.***

St Cuthbert's Island, lying just offshore from Lindisfarne Priory, was used as a retreat by Cuthbert who became the 6th Bishop of Lindisfarne in 685. The unspectacular ruins of a much later medieval chapel survive on the island, possibly overlying the buried remains of an earlier structure dating back to the time of Cuthbert.

St Cuthbert's Island from Lindisfarne.

Dawn over Lindisfarne with Bamburgh Castle on the distant horizon.

Budle Bay forms the southern part of the Lindisfarne Nature Reserve. Its dunes and mudflats are home to a fascinating and internationally important range of plants and birds.

St Aidan's church at Bamburgh, although much altered in subsequent times, seems to date originally from the 12th century. Legends link the site directly with Aidan, who is said to have died on the site in 651. Twelve centuries later, in 1842, the local heroine Grace Darling died of tuberculosis, just 4 years after her famous rescue of shipwrecked sailors off the Bamburgh coast. Her gothic shrine can be visited in St Aidan's churchyard, positioned so as to be visible from ships out to sea. The refurbished Grace Darling Museum, adjacent to the churchyard, is due to open in 2007.

Bamburgh Castle and village under a covering of snow.

The site of Bamburgh Castle may have been occupied continuously since pre-Roman times, and is without doubt one of the most important places in the history of Northumberland. It was from here in the mid 6th century that Ida governed his kingdom of Bernicia, giving rise to the dynasty that would create the magnificent early medieval kingdom of Northumbria, stretching from the Humber to the Forth. The present castle dates from the late 11th century: the magnificent great keep, which dominates the site, was probably added in the 1150s. The castle was much altered in the 18th and 19th centuries, but survives, nevertheless, as a spectacular reminder of Northumberland's eventful ancient history.

Bamburgh Castle from Harkness Rocks.

Owned by the National Trust since 1925, the Farne Islands have a unique historic and natural environment all of their own. The 28 islands (some of which are submerged at high tide) lie from 2 to 5 miles off the coast. St Cuthbert set up a hermitage on Inner Farne, dying here in 687 after which the island became a place of pilgrimage throughout medieval times. St Cuthbert's church on Inner Farne dates back to the late 14th century, though it appears to incorporate masonry from an earlier structure. A second church, St Mary's, stood nearby but has now all but disappeared: slight traces of it are incorporated within the National Trust visitor centre. The lighthouse on Longstone Island, built in 1826, was home to the Darlings, and it was here that those rescued by Grace and her father from the wrecked SS Forfarshire were brought on the morning of 8th September 1838.

Longstone Lighthouse, Farne Islands.

Guillemots.

The Farne Islands are one of Europe's most important bird sanctuaries. Nearly 300 different species of birds have been recorded here, but the islands are best known for the 20 or so species of sea birds that nest here each year. These include puffins, guillemots, razorbills, cormorants, shags, eider ducks, fulmars, gulls, kittiwakes, oystercatchers and terns. Be warned that some of these birds seem to enjoy dive-bombing human visitors! About 1200 Atlantic grey seal pups are born on the Outer Farnes each autumn: the seal colony here is one of the most important in Britain.

Seahouses had a harbour in medieval times, but its present harbour was built in the late 18th century when it was a busy little fishing port, exporting fish, lime and grain. The harbour was further modified and expanded in the 1880s, when 300 fishing boats were based here. It is claimed that Seahouses produced the world's first kipper, the accidental result of some herring having been left overnight in a smoky storeroom! Today, the local economy is based largely on tourism, with boat trips to the Farne Islands always popular.

Seahouses.

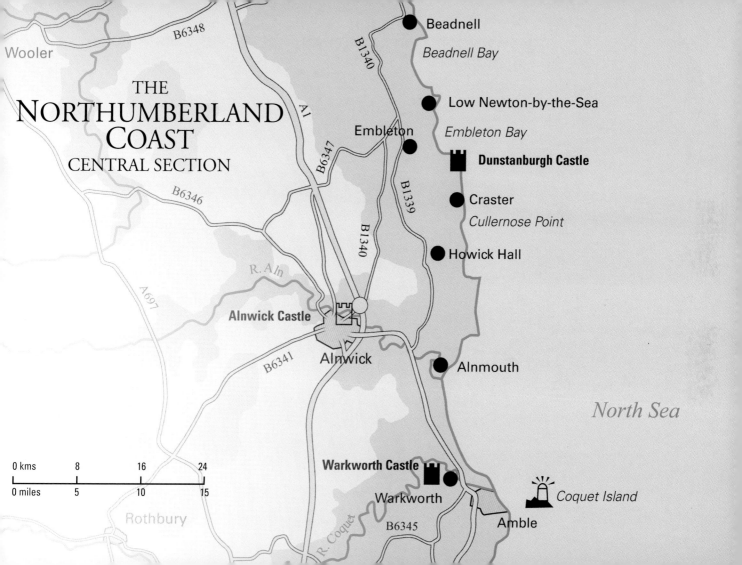

THE
Northumberland Coast
CENTRAL SECTION

Wooler

B6348

B1340

Beadnell

Beadnell Bay

Low Newton-by-the-Sea

Embleton Bay

Embleton

Dunstanburgh Castle

A1

B6347

B1339

Craster

Cullernose Point

B6346

B1340

Howick Hall

R. Aln

A697

Alnwick Castle

B6341

Alnwick

Alnmouth

North Sea

| 0 kms | 8 | 16 | 24 |
| 0 miles | 5 | 10 | 15 |

Warkworth Castle

Warkworth

Coquet Island

Rothbury

B6345

Amble

R. Coquet

St Ebba's chapel at Beadnell, of 13th century date, once served a small monastic community here. Sadly there is little of this left to see, in contrast to the massive late 18th century limekilns which dominate the picturesque little harbour. Originally built to produce lime for export from the harbour, these kilns fell out of use in the 1820s, after which they were adapted for the curing of herrings.

Above: **Beadnell Harbour.**

Right: **Dawn over Beadnell looking towards Dunstanburgh Castle.**

Low Newton, with Dunstanburgh Castle on the distant horizon.

Evening sun over Embleton Bay and Dunstanburgh Castle.

Dunstanburgh Castle, dating from about 1315, encloses an area of about 4.5 hectares, making it the largest castle in Northumberland. However, it played no great role in Northumbrian history, was in ruins by the close of the Wars of the Roses in 1485, and was abandoned for good by the mid 16th century.

Craster, famous for its kippers, was a busy fishing village by the early 17th century. Its present harbour dates from 1910.

*Above: **Craster.***

*Left: **Dunstanburgh Castle from the south.***

At Cullernose Point, 1km south of Craster, the Whin Sill forms a dramatic sea cliff, providing a fine nesting site for seabirds.

Howick has been owned by the Grey family since 1319. Howick Hall was built, on the site of an earlier house, for Sir Henry Grey in 1782. It was partly remodelled in 1928 following a serious fire which destroyed much of the interior. Today, most of the house is unoccupied, but plans are being developed to open part of it to the public. The magnificent Howick Hall gardens are open to the public through spring, summer and autumn. The gardens include many lovely old hardwood trees planted by Charles, the second Earl Grey, who was Prime Minister in the 1830s. Visitors to the garden can also visit the Earl Grey teahouse, and learn about the origin of Earl Grey tea.

The large timber cross on Church Hill, Alnmouth, marks the approximate location of St Waleric's Chapel, built in the 12th century, probably on the site of a much earlier Christian establishment of considerable significance. Church Hill used to be on the same side of the river as Alnmouth, but the river was diverted following the great storm of Christmas 1806, leaving the site of the old chapel in splendid isolation. Alnmouth was an important port from medieval times through until the early 19th century, but the harbour began silting up after the 1806 storm, gradually becoming less of a trading port and more of a fishing harbour. Today, the picturesque village and beautiful beach are much loved by tourists.

*Above: **Alnmouth.***
*Left: **Alnmouth and the mouth of River Aln from Church Hill.***

Fortified bridge, Warkworth.

Warkworth has a history stretching back to the 8th century, when land and a church here were given to the monks of Lindisfarne by King Ceolwulf. The site of this early church is now occupied by the Church of St Laurence. The great castle dates originally from the 12th century: its magnificent keep, combining military strength with grand and comfortable accommodation, was completed in the late 14th century at which time it was amongst the grandest buildings in the whole of Britain. Warkworth Bridge, a very rare form of bridge with a fortified gateway, also dates from the 14th century. The village grew up in the space between the castle and the river, and many fascinating historic buildings still survive here, as does the medieval pattern of long strips or 'burgage plots' extending behind properties built to face onto the main street.

The keep, Warkworth Castle.

Amble, at the mouth of the Coquet just 2km from Warkworth, was only a small village prior to the building of its harbour in the 1840s. Today it is a pleasant small town with a very popular marina, a family-run business with 250 berths.

Coquet Island may have been a monastic site as early as the 7th century. From the 11th century, a monastic cell of Tynemouth Priory was located here, to which a substantial defensible tower was added in the 15th century. The little island is dominated by its lighthouse, built in 1841 on the remains of the medieval tower: its first keeper was William Darling, elder brother of Grace. Today, Coquet Island is an RSPB nature reserve, providing a safe haven for tens of thousands of seabirds including terns which fly here from Africa each year to nest.

THE
NORTHUMBERLAND
COAST
SOUTHERN SECTION

Druridge Bay

North Sea

Morpeth

A697

A1

A1068

A1337

A1068

A189

A197

R. Wansbeck

● Newbiggin-by-the-Sea

Ashington

R. Blyth

A189

Blyth

● Seaton Sluice

A193

St Mary's Lighthouse

● Whitley Bay

0 kms   8   16   24

0 miles   5   10   15

● Cullercoats

NEWCASTLE UPON TYNE

A19

Tynemouth Castle & Priory

North Shields ●

Druridge Bay stretches in a single, glorious 10km sweep of beautiful white sand from Hauxley in the north to Cresswell in the south. Back in the 20th century the landscape surrounding the Bay was scarred by open cast coal mining, but some 235 acres have now been restored as wildlife areas with lakes, reed beds and woodland. The dunes fringing the beach represent an important ecological habitat, including some 300 species of wild plants. The bay provides a winter refuge for birds from northern Europe and Russia, and is visited by many others on their annual migrations from the Arctic and Scandinavia to Africa. The Druridge Bay Country Park visitor centre presents much fascinating information about the bay, and there are trails which focus on local geology, archaeology and ecology.

Blyth had a port in the 12th century, but only became significant in the 18th century as the port was developed for the export of coal: by the 1960s Blyth exported more coal than any other European port. Sadly, the local economy was decimated by the late 20th century decline in coal mining and shipbuilding.

Above: **Staithes, Blyth Harbour.**
Left: **Fishing coble, Newbiggin-by-the-Sea.**

Seaton Sluice is a small village with a fascinating industrial heritage, having been developed by the Delaval family of nearby Seaton Delaval for the export of coal, salt, glass bottles and other goods during the 18th and 19th centuries. In 1764 a new harbour mouth ('The Cut') was blasted through solid rock – an impressive engineering achievement that greatly increased the efficiency of the harbour.

*Above: **Looking towards 'The Cut', Seaton Sluice.***
*Right: **Harbour, Seaton Sluice.***

St Mary's Lighthouse, Whitley Bay.

Lifeboat station, Cullercoats.

Cullercoats was associated with the salt trade in the 17th century, but by the mid 18th century existed as a small but well-respected fishing village – described in 1749 as the best fish market in north-east England. In Victorian times it became a popular dormitory for Newcastle, expanding northwards along the coast to form the larger town of Whitley Bay which itself became a major seaside resort enjoyed by people from Tyneside and further afield. The impressive lighthouse on St Mary's Island dates from 1898 and remained operational until 1984. Today it is a visitor centre, with visitors able to climb its 137 steps and enjoy splendid views of the coast.

The church of St George, Cullercoats, a memorial to the fifth Duke of Northumberland provided by his son and completed in 1884, stands proudly over the windswept Long Sands.

Looking across Long Sands towards Cullercoats from Tynemouth.

Tynemouth probably had a monastery by the mid 7th century, and certainly by 800 when it was sacked by Vikings. Little is known of the next couple of centuries, but the monastery was refounded in the 11th century and functioned through until the Dissolution in 1539. The most spectacular surviving remains date from the late 12th century. The site was a fortress as well as a monastery, its medieval castle and defences, in combination with the naturally defensible nature of the site, made it pretty much impregnable. However, Scottish raids during the Border Wars did take cause damage, leading to the construction of the great gatehouse in the early 15th century.

*Above: **North Pier and Priory, Tynemouth.***
*Left: **Tynemouth Priory.***

For most of its history, Tynemouth village existed as an unremarkable little settlement along the road leading to the priory and castle. However, after the coming of the railway in the mid 19th century it developed as a popular dormitory town and holiday resort.

Following numerous unfortunate and sometimes tragic incidents on the treacherous rocks off Tynemouth, the nation's first Volunteer Life Brigade was formed here and the Watch Club House was constructed as its headquarters in 1887. This distinctive timber building is now a museum, presenting information about the history of ships and shipping on the Tyne, including details of several local maritime disasters.

North Shields is first recorded as a fishing village associated with Tynemouth Priory in the early 13th century. It remained as little more than a village for half a millennium, but began expanding after 1750 through its association with coal mining, shipbuilding and shipping. Sadly, in more recent times, the town has suffered through the decline in these traditional industries. Nevertheless, even though much has been lost to recent redevelopment, a number of fine churches and public buildings do survive from its heyday and its maritime traditions are continued through the North Shields Fish Quay, the Royal Quays Marina, and the Port of Tyne.

North Shields Fish Quay.

The watchtower at the mouth of the River Tyne, North Shields.